Take that, Batman. Elizabeth Scanlon gives The Dark Knight the finger and it's a beautiful thing because these poems in *Whosoever Whole* are the real superheroes. These poems have the power to embrace and heal the rotting and the hurt and the glorious joy in the Gotham of your heart. I'm talking: they will provide a quietness the instant that you read them and then long after you have read them. Because *time* is a personified swimmer wearing a Speedo hurtling past the breaking waves. Because *beauty* is headed out the door. Because you get to play mini-golf under a LOVE sculpture on the Winter Solstice. It is this kind of joyful quiet that persists. This is the *super-hero human-hero* power of this book, of these poems. The joyous quiet. Scanlon's poems are meditations and meditative and *Whosoever Whole* is a collection of poems that is monk-like — naked, on a boulder in the middle of some clean, cold river, getting as close to the quiet as a woman who is good with a knife because she can peel the apple in one long peel. *Whosoever Whole* is that one long peel that keeps on going into the dark night making us complete, completing the uncompleted, into a stillness of delight, that simply put, makes one feel good.

—Matthew Lippman, author of *We Are All Sleeping with Our Sneakers On*

Whosoever Whole is a sly, winking book of magic. It threatens to read your browser history and luxuriates in the chaos of a South Philly bus ride. Elizabeth's poems are warm and funny, but always with a sharp edge that takes on pregnancy, parenting, and getting older with a punk energy that kept me smiling. It's a fun, real, raw book that I can't wait to keep coming back to.

—Warren C. Longmire, author of *Bird/Diz: An Erased History of Bebop*

In Elizabeth Scanlon's *Whosoever Whole*, an ardent voice cuts over our commodity-driven culture's insistence on endless striving and complacency amid ecological and systemic collapse. These poems call out the epochal crises that threaten our survival while remaining deftly attuned to the

rage, desire, frustration, and conviction that keep one from capitulating to a wonder-bereft society. Spending "hours on the internet / looking for something to hurt you" and feeling adrift in this craven, late capitalist reality may be unavoidable, but Scanlon adeptly orients us toward what's remarkable: "There is / spirit, and that is boundless." With the intimacy of a beloved linking their arm with yours on the walk home after a long night, the speaker wryly reminds us of our interconnectedness ("My guy, our fates are combining / all the time"), channeling how wild and precarious it is to be alive and the reasons to continue: "I can only believe / that the revolution is still coming / and we will be here for it."
—Alina Pleskova, author of *Toska*

Whosoever Whole

Cover art: *Original Teeth* by Joey Sweeney
Cover design by Joey Sweeney
Cover typeface: Neue Kabel
Interior design by Laura Joakimson
Interior typeface: Optima and Perpetua

Library of Congress Cataloging-in-Publication Data

Names: Scanlon, Elizabeth, 1973- author.
Title: *Whosoever Whole* / Elizabeth Scanlon.
Description: Oakland, California : Omnidawn Publishing, 2024. | Summary:
"Poems that offer an anti-capitalist consideration of life and selfhood
for women in contemporary society. The poetry in Elizabeth Scanlon's
Whosoever Whole asks how we arrive at and nurture a sense of self amid a
culture that wants us only to consume. Navigating the fractal and often
fractured experiences of a citizen, a parent in the time of climate
change, and a woman in an embattled era, Scanlon invites the reader into
an interior space filled with anger, joy, wonder, and hope. Employing
metaphor and metonymy, these poems portray a series of courageous
portraits of the many faces a woman must wear to survive in today's
culture. *Whosoever Whole* is an anti-capitalist love song to all who
refuse to be torn apart by the market valuation of their lives."
Provided by publisher.

Identifiers: LCCN 2024003125 | ISBN 9781632431295 (trade paperback)
Subjects: BISAC: POETRY / American / General | POETRY / Women Authors |
LCGFT: Poetry.
Classification: LCC PS3619.C265 W48 2024 | DDC 811/.6--dc23/eng/20240129
LC record available at https://lccn.loc.gov/2024003125

Published by Omnidawn Publishing, Oakland, California
www.omnidawn.com
10 9 8 7 6 5 4 3 2 1
ISBN: 978-1-63243-129-5

Whosoever Whole

Elizabeth Scanlon

Omnidawn Publishing
Oakland California
2024

Table of Contents

1.

Whole

The tissues taken, do you resent them,
and which, the takers or the things,
the wisdom teeth, the placenta, the hanks of hair —
a small part does, some scab of soul
wishes to be whole as a wolf in the woods.
Those drabs were mine.
I understand the hoarder,
the bag lady, the Lear
limping along in a big box store,
even as I look away —
there's shame in wanting.
It's such a mess. How do we
unlearn the drive for more?
We've never not loved excess.

Post-post-internet

When did you begin to hear it, the little radio
that never turns off, broadcasting night and day?

Post-post-internet, all my eye problems went away,
they weren't dry anymore or running tears either,
post-post-internet I remembered what it was like
to wake and not know what happened in the night.

Some spill of watercolor diffuses
in the glass —
        watch the dye
               spool out —

those who have never cleaned think
every old thing must be replaced.
Just because you've never used a sponge
doesn't mean it's not a real thing
that works.

Laying cheek to table is soothing.
The grain of the wood.

The baby-having part of life,
the storybooks and butterfat part,
passed in so much money panic, illness,
and weariness, I barely remember it —

        we used to count age in weeks.

The skylight I didn't notice until it leaked.

Who Will You Be?

The scariest thing to find
in any room is another person.
My hallucinations tell me this,

also, the news, or whatever it is
we call the reports from every medium.
We need a new word

for ghost, for news,
also one for *that is nice I don't care*
also one for *that is terrifying who are you*

I'm my favorite monster:
the papier-mâché mask has all my features, only
bigger, much bigger, more rageful.

I think I am getting better at being in the world –
Call forth Lazarus from his grave
I died so many times trying not to frighten you.

Going to bed shouldn't feel like defeat
                    (I am getting better at being in the world)
You will see me when you least expect it.

Whosoever

What is this a culture of?
We do not ask enough.

Car culture failed —
Suburbia failed —
too much for too little —

it is another today today and we know
the founding fathers were liars.

*We have to consciously study how to be tender
with each other,* Audre said.
Where is that school?

Who will you be?

The offices of the principals play blameless & beige.
The receptionists had little pink pads that said
while you were out

this dream city of gloss & strass bled
into sprawl, it was already failing in the '80s
when it was dominant but diseased, like CEOs everywhere.

I know it is too much to say so!
(The heart is a muted trumpet.)

Still life: lay your burden down in the room
quietly alone with your gun & your car keys,
American,
probing the wound of your own mess —

I call and call, you never answer.

The Hope

In 1958, the Hope Diamond was mailed
to the Smithsonian in a plain brown box.
I don't imagine they left it on the doorstep,
but still, that's a lot of faith in the government.

They say it's cursed but then again others say
the story was cooked up by gem dealers
to increase its allure: a dangerous beauty.
Talk your trash.

The only hope there is for money
is to have so much of it you never have
to talk about it again.

What It's Like

You're right, I'll never know
what it's like to live with me.
Even though I've been doing it
all this time.

A housemate once said
I spat the same sound every night
when I brushed my teeth.
Imagine her listening.

I do have an odd habit of humming
the first few bars of "America"
when trying to remember
what I meant to do next.

I wonder if my son
will hear that song years from now
and feel some kind of way about it
and not know why.

One thing you know

about a woman who can peel an apple in one long coil
is that she's good with a knife, good
at staying her hand from cutting too deep,
another thing you know is that the apple
is smooth and true, picked
by feel not looks. She hardly looks
at the thing unspooling in her hand.
She will give you a slice you didn't ask for
and eat her own, held between thumb and blade.

Self-Portrait as Ghost

I have lain in the dark of the folds of the dresses
I made, tiny-waisted, swiss dot or deep green velvet, rickracked
and flounced, bundled in tissue and kept
in your hope chest though there's no future
in which you or I will fit them;
I am   the aroma that clings to them,
though impossible, forty years gone,
ancient as a pharaoh the loss of form but still, molecular,
indefatigable, perceptible, a musk
in the seam of the armpit, a *Rive Gauche* chrome rose
entwined along the neckline, dust of skin and dirt milled
too fine to see; the fibers I am
of the fabric are stiffening for want of wear   I am,
I never imagined these costumes of ladyness
would last so long, thought I would have worn them
out, as I would had I time,
but nestled in among them   I am

Acceptance Speech

It is because I know I cannot be everywhere at once
that I know my tomb is empty & that Death
made me a maudlin kind of child from the start,
always happier on the verge of tears, rapt,
atingle with the snuffing sense,
making everyone so uncomfortable.

Someone taught you how to cut your toenails,
someone knew before you did,
intimately and precisely,
how the corner of the left big toe tends
to ingrow & so to be extra vigilant there.
You don't remember it, or who,
but it's unlikely no one ever had your toes
on their to-do list.
When you grant acknowledgment,
when you stand on your own two feet,
there is no way to thank everyone.

No one plans to live past thirty-five,
we're all surprised to be here even if
you were a good kid and never made anyone wish
you were never born.

It's more comfortable
to ignore the body even as it demands
to be made more comfortable,
easier not to think about sex & snot,
sad for the lost euphoria of that one good high,
the walking the whole city the way home one,
the perfect sun rising, not one single moment
of anything but bliss.

That one memory that gave rise
to eight thousand awful ones.

But in praise of graves:
they allow you to visit them
without comment, they bear
your morose moods, glow
in the sunshine,
they are so solid.

The world is full of broken people,
every bus a Ouija board
on which you surf the speakings
of the departed.

Glide over *Good-Bye* —

pocket the planchette,
stop treating yourself like a servant,
as do I, always wondering why
I'm not faster or more grateful —

someday I will be done searching,
I will stop typing your name over & over
in different combinations to see
if you have left any trail

any indication of where not to go.

Spring Wish

Years ago
it was May
I was huge
seven months in
wrapped in a shawl
walking to work
when I saw them
in the square
we talked about crystals
and some blooming trees
and when I said
I'd been feeling so clumsy
they said why
I replied
because I'm pregnant
They said oh!
I hadn't noticed
and it was
a wonderful thing
to go unnoticed
having felt so awkward
and conspicuous
not even knowing
that I had been wishing
to be unseen a little bit
not asked about
my future plans
or baby names
and I laughed
and all
our bellies shook.

Summer Mother, 6 AM

Who holds the myth
that summer is carefree
when indeed it's just the bright leaves
returning

that obscures the view
of the skeletons;
wanting to replace all the lost things
just like the leaves returning to the trees,

where are those green jade teardrops
stolen from my mother's ears?
I am the god looking down
at five suns in a bowl,

five perfect gold yolks
suspended in their own cosmos,
deciding whether to smash them
or fry them whole.

For the Decades

In the beginning, in single digits
I was the Great Depression and you
were the Revolution,
your tens were my eighties and so on
and to be a teenager in what is to come
is a thing I can hardly imagine
and I have imagination to spare
but what is there to believe about
our poisonous air and our fractal touch
our digital renderings of buildings
that don't exist to contain classes
that won't happen
but I can only believe
that the revolution is still coming
and we will be here for it
future generations will
not believe it was as bad as we say
because it is ludicrous,
what was done for money
and not done for people
and that there was a time when
owning houses was a thing
people signed their lives away for,
my love, my baby,
may we never gloss the crimes
of this era

Devotion

Your mother is a creep.
Everyone's mother is a creep;
we have envelopes of your teeth
in our bedside drawers,
clippings of your hair.
We check your browser history.
Listen to your footsteps in the night
back and forth to the bathroom,
listen even harder if you're in there too long.
The self is a recent construct, relatively;
a hundred years ago there were far fewer
ways to say *mine*. Your clothes we sniff.
Try to guess what you want for dinner,
what you had for lunch.
In the *I and Thou* model,
all meaning stems from relationships,
the other the stand-in for the God,
who is always absent.
We try to take your picture
when you're not looking.
Everything we warn you about,
we are.

Figures

Most of cooking is waiting for change to occur;
water softens the rice, chicken skin crisping.

My son does his science homework at the table, questions
about physical or chemical properties.

A physical change doesn't alter the substance.
In chemical change, there is a reaction,

a new substance is formed,
energy is either given off or absorbed.

I think of the Novembers of his baby years,
not very long ago.

They were cold.

How is your Anthropocene going?
How many more days of collapse
do you have in you?

Home School

for 2020

It is not that I that I dread
being stuck with you it is that
I do not want you to be stuck
with me and at precisely the moment
when your world should be getting bigger
for it to contract so feels especially
foreign. The parents of a five-year-old
I know say the same, the daughter
of a recent retiree likewise,
the polyamorous, certainly, and them
that rely on an audience all the more.
What will make us enough.
I will continue my French lessons
and plot the escape while you
surpass me in maths I've never known.
May we arrive at a place beyond testing.

Winter Solstice Mini Golf

It was 70 degrees on the 21st of December;
everyone had lost their mind. Sweating Santas
rang bells and shook their asses around kettles
like some parking lot ritual and Starbucks
had a run on those grande peppermint mocha whatevers,
iced, double whip, so the hyper-caffeinated shoppers
roaming the streets in bare arms were at a psychedelic level
of stimulation for a day on which there would be
still very few hours.
                        My son and I putt-putted through
the *LOVE* sculpture, under the Chinatown Arch,
where you're meant to make a wish,
through Boathouse Row and back to the Bell.
I wished we would live out our natural lives.
The shadows across the green were long
as leafless branches.
We were equal parts dark and light.

2.

The Arrangement

In a trance I saw the moment when you left
the person who was once yourself and,
in just the same way you look back
at a broom-clean room you rented, with some sorrow
and some relief, shut the door. You don't live there
anymore, and its drafts and bugs won't bother you.
Where does medical waste go?
Tumors, tonsils, all the tubes of blood
coffined in shipping containers on flatbed trucks
or seaports awaiting their immolation, yes,
we know they're turned to ash but then, but then —
there is no destruction of matter.

Materiality

Looking up is a physical act—
choreograph your seeing,
notice the seams in the wall,
the shadow of mesh tape spackled over
but not quite thoroughly enough
to hide that the house is held together
the same way a shoebox diorama is,
a habitat depicted in miniature. Homeowners
like to think, I suppose, that their bricks and mortar
protect them, but

If you ask, hey,
where did that money come from?
They might say I earned it
or if they have a pang of honesty,
my family gave it to me,
but almost never does anyone answer:
because someone just liked the looks of me
some grandma or boss man or deity said,
yeah, that one.

A Myth

Scarcity said to hoard while you're strong
so that when weakness arrives no harm will come
to you. But whose failure arrives on time?
I know exactly what's wrong with me.
Too little nudity, too much forced air,
too long on the bus without getting anywhere.
You can't think your way out of anxiety any more
than you can drink yourself out of thirst
and here's the loop, the hook, the thing that keeps you
coming back around –
there's a crime in believing there's a way to prepare
and that those who didn't deserve what they got.

My guy, our fates are combining
all the time. Purity another myth and who knows
what's in that dinner you paid too much for.
It may sate your hunger but give you a rash;
it may be the flesh of a lost god
prowling the bottom of the sea
looking for one honest man.
Eat up, dip it in butter,
there is no cure.

Astrophysicists in Spain

Have proposed that the center of the Milky Way
smells like raspberries and tastes like rum;

they have observed a dirt cloud
around Sagittarius B2, very near the heart

of the galaxy, and found a predominance
of ethyl formate, which to the nose

of a perfumer would suggest raspberry
or to the tongue, rum;

it occurs naturally in the bodies of ants,
which makes me wonder, do ants taste like rum?

How many would you need to pesto
to appreciate the flavor?

It is maybe gluttonous to find this so cheerful,
but there is no sin in space, which is why

we want to go there.
It may be that the astrophysicists,

learned as they are,
knew that we'd take the bait

and ask no further
about the location of the heart.

Pieces of the Picture

A flag rippling in the wind
sounds like fire, a strong bonfire,
the kind you think might leap
the bounds and singe the nearby trees,
and why wouldn't it
                              sound that way
                              burn that way
Air moving through
vocal cords is a scream. Air blares
a horn. The wind flaps the laundry on the line.
You know something about where you are
when you see laundry on a line.

Self-assessment

I thought about
all the things I might buy
and then didn't
I thought about
how when you used to
undo your jeans they'd fall
straight to the floor
and now they don't
everything is tight all over
that's just the style
that's just a body
it's been that way for ages
it's still uncomfortable
Can you feel your liver
Can you feel the love tonight
Can you feel barometric pressure
How about now?

Mood

It's insulting to be told not to be sad
when there's no recourse,

to be told everything
will be ok.

It is good I don't drive;
it would be satisfying

to speed away. Cars are being used
for murder more often than ever before.

Those who lived right before the car had no idea
how utterly everything was about to change.

You might live your whole life this way,
sitting in a tree if you're of a tree-climbing people.

Waiting for someone to turn you in
if you feel guilty.

Cleaning Windows

Remember when
they were building
that building
It felt like forever
Remember when
that was an empty lot
It was like that forever
And even now
when we walk by it
my peripheral vision
is confused
by the walls there
instead of scrub grass,
the solid brick stack
taking up the air
we were used to
and assumed would stay
but that is a city virtue,
that refusal
to be unchanged.

We are not volcanoes

Whose pain do we doubt?
Our own irritation is blinding, I know.
The creditors are the only ones who call every day.
We gave up on landlines because of telemarketers
but now the debt collectors are in your pocket
and we can't quit them because we're all they've got,
and the connection gets thinner and thinner
every time we think we have to have something.
The ground is heavy with us.
On my phone, a GIF of lava,
rolling and mumbling like it's waking
from a bad dream, is it helpful to see it illustrated onscreen?
We are not volcanoes.
We don't walk around bleeding
while we're looking at our phones trying to figure out
whose number that might be
or do we, and maybe this oozing earth
is scarred beyond compassion,
is the guy on the street we look away from because his pain
will be the same as yesterday's, only more.
It's too much and we're tired of owing –
even if you could open your gut
like an oval vinyl coin purse on a little ball chain
and spill out gold it wouldn't be enough – and your belly feels full
of bus tokens, heavy and out of use, you search yourself
because you forgot you were robbed – we're bound
to do a lot of checking, rummaging through all the pockets,
every organ maybe the one in which we put that receipt.

Compassion

Not a hundred or a thousand
but hundreds of thousands of starlings
in the stand of bamboo next to the house she rented –

It sounds like a fairy tale
until she elaborates
on the tsunami of bird shit they produce
The stench of it and how it singes
the paint off nearby cars

How like your refusal to believe
the birds hiding in the woods
The problem much worse than it sounds
Corrosive and not at all funny

Man with Big Stick

He was dressed for the gym and shouldered
a heavy backpack, he was doing squats
and quad stretches at the corner
of the square, could have been mistaken
for a student had he not been yelling at no one
and carrying a Very Large Stick —
almost a log, a branch as tall as he was,
as big around as his arm, felled
from one of the old trees during a week of storms.
He used it as a free weight, an épée, and then,
a wand, waving it with great difficulty as he bellowed
I am your father —
see how close passersby come to him,
completely unaware
before veering in a wide arc,
unsure if this is performance art
or a potential bludgeoning —
he announced he was Spartacus
before laying his prize down on the ground
and jumping over it, back and forth,
like basic training, like a wedding day.

All the Water in the World

There is the same amount of water on Earth
      as there was when the Earth was formed.
         It's just that we're ruining it.

If you can move water efficiently you can control
      the desert, which is a weird goal.
         Water can dissolve

more substances than any other liquid,
      including sulfuric acid.
         Take that, Batman.

Superheroes were always threatened with
      acid-centric plans; remember?
         The solution was much simpler.

Do you know how many aloe plants I killed
      by loving them wrong?
         Too much water.

It takes 1,008 gallons of water
      to make one gallon of wine.
         Sedate the thirsty.

I knew a man who almost perfected a bean
      that could grow in arid climates,
         his goal was, honestly,

to end world hunger, even under capitalism.
      He dreamed. He fell from a window
         before his research was complete.

I want to believe that like the boat upon the water
      that so loved the bigness of the sea,

he knew the great swell
in the going.

3.

For You

You have a book
that explains time
in your glovebox.
I'll ride shotgun
I'll fix your clock
and balance the tomato pie
till we get to the ocean.
It's been ages
wondering how
all these people
got all these houses
though really,
we have known.
It wasn't work.
You say how do I
I say no one does
It is the generations
Let's get out of here

For Chico with Love & Squalor

I've had just enough
to know what I'm missing
in education & dollars & love,
in tongues & guts
& while California offers
its platter of olives & grapes
there's a phone ringing down the hall
in the communal TV room of the east coast
that will not let me rest.
The asterisk that appears
at the end of a line of fine print
to indicate that there's something more
you should know, some whispered aside,
insider information, that asterisk
looks like an asshole, or the North Star.

This Thing

You're taking a lot
of pictures of yourself
because you know
it's almost over,
this Beauty thing,
the thing they said
you had going for you
all along when really
what good did it ever do
but now
that you see it
heading for the door
It feels different
feels like the friend you didn't know
was at the crowded party,
too noisy & hot,
until you're halfway out the door
the car already waiting
& so say hello & goodbye
all in one breath.

For the Future

Don't allow the fortune teller to tell you anything.
Even if you proceed in perfect disbelief
you will never get the words out of your ears
and if she says your throat will someday close
you'll think of it with every cold,
every kernel of corn.
I know words,
how unleaving they are,
how porous the intended vessel.

Drumcliffe Churchyard

We went to see Yeats and waded through
stone after stone bearing our own names.
When they were in Ireland, the bloodbearers
who came before, in Sligo or Ballina,
those bricklayers and beadcounters, they did not
know or care what would become of us,
the later-thans, which we forgive.
Are you thinking of your great-great-grandchildren?
No, you cannot conceive of them.
But what was is as imaginary as what might be.
The ancestors toiled.
They burned their peat and walked.
They sheared the sheep
and slept.

I Call, You Never Answer

Time has always been patriarchal,
nosy, bossy, not very helpful.
The unit in which corrections are measured.
No one has ever called time Mother,
only Father Time, with his long white beard
& scythe, lanky-limbed in that effortless way,
flowing robes to hide the red Speedo
he wears to swim away
past the lifeguards,
out past the break.

Still Life

The chair longs for the table
but someone is always coming between them.
They don't even touch. Or barely, sometimes,
a shoulder-to-shoulder lean, a backwards bump.
The table wears its age better, no surprise,
having been sat upon less. The chair
creaks all the time. Is coming apart at the joints.
Longs for the old club days when,
after closing, they'd stack ass to face
and rest that way till the next day.

Billboard 2: I Love You

(after Zoe Strauss)

The photo of the tattoo as precise
as the tattoo is not: completely.
You can see every mottle of the layers of skin,
a complexion pink and purple, tan and grey,
marbled white like a ham, fine brown hairs
sprouting around the edges of the blue ink,
bleeding dots connected to form the letters.
This was no gun job, this is homemade
or maybe prison-made,
and think of that, the determination;
to get the things, to do the thing. Or maybe
it was a teenage bathroom operation,
like my brother and I did with a sewing needle
and India ink, I punched
that little black heart into his bicep.
Think how many jabs it took.
It shows us to be aqueous; it is floating toward the surface,
emerging from within the liquid center,
a twenty-sided die in the Magic 8 Ball, spinning
a hazy reply to anyone who looks,
who shakes.

Too Sweet

Juice is too much of a good thing,
just eat the orange already.

You spend hours on the internet
looking for something to hurt you

to feel something other than busy.

Slowly

I could hear the roses reaching when I was small,
unfurling like paper crumpled in reverse

my young uncle long ago
with his silky long hair, said once

he was watching his fingernails grow
I didn't know

anything about being high,
it wouldn't have occurred to me

that he was,
or that he was kidding,

I only thought, oh, how good
to be so patient, you see so much.

Awakening

The man was asleep
in the driver's seat
of a beige sedan,
unshaven, balding,
frizzled around the edges
in the way middle age affects;
we did not know he was asleep
and assumed the worst —
why, as little children,
did we leap immediately
to the conclusion
that this was a dead man
before us,
laid out in his car
with the headrest angled just so?
His mouth hung loose,
his crumpled shirt.
He never knew
we mourned him
but I still think of us there,
a semi-circle of congregants
gathered around his window,
clutching dandelions,
gazing in at the ruin.

Never Alone

Is your haunting a good dog,
one who leaves the room when you're doing it?

Or the bad one that knocks over the water glass,
slams into the window jumping at a squirrel?

Do you feel its presence hungering
while you fix your breakfast?

Or does it just rest its head in your lap,
resigned? Oh hound.

Oh lost and found. I cannot know
what became of your parents, your litter.

You're only mine now.

4.

Immunity

Is it out of our system yet,
the apocalypse, the end of days
portrayed on every movie & TV show?
Animals strewn across fields,
cars abandoned, shops ransacked?
A mockup of the real, sad, slow
decline. They started making the zombies
run faster to spice it up.

Is it working its way through our bloodstream –

Do go on, I said,
          to my son describing his video game –

We always wind up in a grocery store
buying too much stuff
& wondering if it is enough.

Do You Think

Will life be long
enough to be all the selves

you've longed for
They'll blame you

no matter what you do
If you smoked or fucked

you were your own undoing
My friend said he always imagined

people did something to deserve
a disease until it was him

We all thought
we were modern

Holding horns to our ears
calling the switchboard

We think it now

Imbolc Comes Around Again

(St. Brigid's Day, February 2)

In the belly of the mother, milk of ewes,
      I dwell in you like a child. Like a seed,
like a cyst. I smith the iron will.
      Crown of lights for you & me.
Everything is haunted. The souls of all the gunshots.
      The wind cries, mice skitter, the trees bend
backwards, the water spins counterclockwise
      because everything is haunted.
I'm weary of grieving the losses. January get away,
      the wind be my door,
Brigid, be a dear and dole the banes upon the cold
      that remains.
The more fierce an animal is, or will be,
      in its maturity, the longer it stays
          vulnerable —
the foal born walking gentle from the start,
      a bear coddled a year or more, and us,
          look at us — barely able to stand
        until called to

Stag in the Cathedral

He looks to his left, then his right.
He climbs the stairs to the altar,
the pews are too small.
The chandeliers mirror his antlers
but look cold without his velvet.
There's gold everywhere,
glinting in the filtered rays,
on the edges of the pages,
the pyx, the font, gold
that became the treasure
of the world more for its
chemical aloofness than its rarity,
it will not rust or crumble,
it will outlast us. That is why
the church collects it,
intimation of life everlasting.
The deer found his way in
and wants out.
We have no idea what is rare.

A Request

To love entirely that which will die

is the work we are set to, knowing

too that to dwell on it is a mistake.

How then to ask and not ask, bleed

but stay clean. I see the shadows

of spots on my hands, I do.

Give me time to figure out what

they are a map of, where this knot-rope

ladder leads. Longevity is not its own

reward; I think, it may mean you walk home

alone in the dark, may mean you are

better with the shield than the sword.

For Easter

In full view of this rising sun, I wish for more,
knowing that I have already wished
so much of my time away,
a dumbass like me! An eater of eggs
who has been mostly happy
beyond explaining while seeming otherwise,
while not deserving it, because who could,
while cancers and starvations rage,
while still living in the hope
of one day waking.
It will be a morning like no other.
I'll ride my bike, I'll eat cheesecake,
maybe at the same time.

That you will lose the most precious thing
over and over, that is life on earth.
That there will be another most precious thing
that you will lose, too,
even after you know it is coming,
just as the oldest person on earth
will have outlived everyone who was alive
at their birth when they go.

I do not know why
there remains in me some child
who flails *no*
in dread at every new task while
another part picks that one up
in a fireman's carry and shushes
I know I know
as we go on about the business
of getting it done.

I am, you are, Lazarus —

Behold me!
Are we not amazed?

By the time the flowers from the bodega
have died, you are done with them.
Praise them with me.
Nothing else so symmetrical
in its timing.

Third & Pine

(a golden shovel)

Leaving the house I
fail to remember where I am,
that is, in the Big Picture, or the
Oneness or whatever, at least
it feels that way. It's difficult
to be wakeful of
purpose, surrounded by men
leaving crumbs where they fall, all
over the damn place. There's no map. I
think of your Tennessee-shaped wine stain, I want
to kiss you there. There is
spirit, and that is boundless,
as opposed to what to do with your time, your love.

Aubade

In the heaven of the martyrs, everyone gets
what they deserve. For the rest of us,
it's more variable. You snore, I obsess —
each to their own worst traits and if the debate
leaves you unable to sleep for hours,
at least I get a head start. Often when dawn teeters
on the edge of the window and you are coming
to bed as I rise, the purple sky is the bruise
of wanting: it lightens quickly but I can still feel
where I've pressed so hard the vessels of night burst
beneath the surface. It may be we promised
all our time in order to find any time at all,
net-fishing our chances to have some sort of life together
before the gains are weighed.

Notes

"Whosoever" quotes Audre Lorde: "We have to consciously study how to be tender with each other until it becomes a habit," from her essay "Eye to Eye" in *Sister Outsider*.

"For Chico with Love & Squalor" takes its title from a phrase in Eve Babitz's *Sex & Rage*.

"Billboard 2: I Love You" is an ekphrastic poem after Zoe Strauss's photograph of the same name.

"Third & Pine" is a golden shovel (with thanks to Terrance Hayes for creating the form). The Frank O'Hara line it draws upon, "I am the least difficult of men, all I want is boundless love," is from "Meditations in an Emergency."

"Imbolc Comes Around Again" refers to the ancient Celtic celebration on February 2nd, also known as St Brigid's Day, halfway between the winter solstice and spring equinox.

Acknowledgments

Many thanks to the editors of the following journals,
in which poems from this collection first appeared:

bedfellows
Bennington Review
The Common
Copper Nickel
diode
The Iowa Review
The Georgia Review
Love's Executive Order
The Normal School
Poetry Ireland
Poetry International
Poetry London
Poetry Northwest
Prolit
Washington Square Review
Wildness

Elizabeth Scanlon is the author of *Lonesome Gnosis* (Horsethief Books), *The Brain Is Not the United States / The Brain Is the Ocean* (The Head & The Hand Press), and *Odd Regard* (ixnay press). Her poems have appeared in many magazines, including *Boston Review*, *Bennington Review*, *Poetry London*, and *Poetry Ireland*. She is the Editor-in-Chief of *The American Poetry Review* and lives in Philadelphia, PA.

Whosoever Whole
by Elizabeth Scanlon
Cover art: *Original Teeth* by Joey Sweeney
Cover design by Joey Sweeney
Cover typeface: Neue Kabel
Interior design by Laura Joakimson
Interior typeface: Optima and Perpetua

Printed in the United States
by Books International,
Dulles, Virginia on Acid Free Archival Quality Recycled Paper

Publication of this book was made possible in part by gifts from Katherine & John
Gravendyk in honor of Hillary Gravendyk,
Francesca Bell, Mary Mackey, and The New Place Fund

Omnidawn Publishing Oakland, California
Staff and Volunteers, Spring 2024
Rusty Morrison & Laura Joakimson, co-publishers
Rob Hendricks, editor for Omniverse, poetry & fiction,
& post-pub marketing
Jeffrey Kingman, copy editor
Sharon Zetter, poetry editor & book designer
Anthony Cody, poetry editor
Liza Flum, poetry editor
Kimberly Reyes, poetry editor
Elizabeth Aeschliman, fiction & poetry editor
Jennifer Metsker, marketing assistant
Katie Tomzynski, marketing assistant
Sophia Carr, production assistant